on duty

LIFE IN
ARMY BASIC TRAINING

Gene Gartman

HIGH
interest
books

Children's Press
A Division of Grolier Publishing
New York / London / Hong Kong / Sydney
Danbury, Connecticut

Book Design: Lisa Quattlebaum
Contributing Editor: Mark Beyer

Photo Credits: side bar © Superstock; pp. 5, 7, 22, 29, 36 © Annie Griffiths
Belt/Corbis; pp. 10, 25, 31, 34 © U.S. Army; pp. 37, 39, 40 courtesy of the
Wilson family; pp. 14, 17, 22 © Leif Skoogfors/Corbis; p. 19 © Kevin
Fleming/Corbis; p. 23 © The Military Picture Library/Corbis; p. 26, 29, 33 ©
Corbis.

Visit Children's Press on the Internet at:
http://publishing.grolier.com

Cataloging-in-Publication Data

Gartman, Gene
    Life in Army basic training / Gene Gartman.
    p. cm.—(On duty)
    Includes bibliographical references and index.
    Summary: This book describes U.S. Army basic training, from orienta-
    tion for new recruits to graduation.
    ISBN 0-516-23347-5 (lib. bdg.)   0-516-23547-8 (pbk.)
    1. Basic training (Military education) – United States –
Juvenile literature   2. United States. Army – Military life –
Juvenile literature   [1. United States. Army – Military life]
    I. Title   II. Series
    2000
355.5'4'0973—dc21

CONTENTS

Introduction

Basic training has always been very important to military life. People who join the military and enter basic training are called recruits. Recruits take basic training in the air force, army, navy, marines, and the coast guard. Not every basic training program is the same. This book describes what happens during U.S. Army basic training.

Basic training takes just eight weeks to teach recruits what they need to know about military life. As a recruit, you will have a chance to meet people and make new friends. Also, you will learn skills such as first aid, weapons training, and self-discipline. These are skills most people never learn. You will learn how to defend yourself and do things you have never done before. You will go through physical training, hand

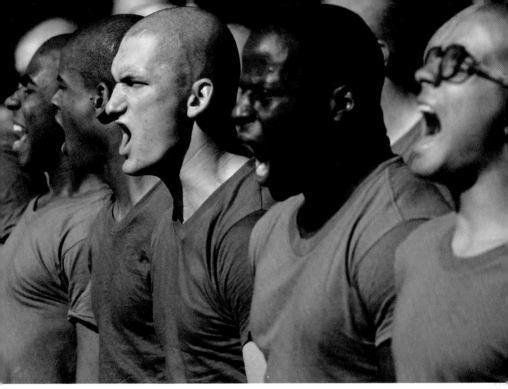

In only eight weeks, these raw recruits will become United States soldiers.

grenade training, and teamwork training.

After just eight weeks, you will have made the move from being a young high school student to being a lean, strong, well-trained soldier. The experiences from basic training will always stay with you. They will help you save lives and will keep you alive. These experiences will carry you through your entire service with the U.S. Army.

Army Reception

JOINING THE MILITARY

Before you leave home for basic training, you have to enlist in one of the armed forces branches. During enlistment, you are given a choice of assignments. Your assignment depends on what you want to do in the military. What you do in the military often can carry over to a job after you leave the military. There are many different kinds of assignments you can choose. Some options are medical training, police training, and computer training. The training for these specialties takes place all over the world. The military recruiter will help you decide which assignment to choose. The recruiter will ask you questions about your goals in life. The recruiter also will ask you why you want to join the military.

Each day in basic training begins with exercise.

A Myth About Basic Training

The idea that basic training "breaks you down" and then "builds you into a fighting machine" comes from movies and television. They show recruits being humiliated. They seem to tell the public that recruits must be alone and fight their way for acceptance. These stories are not true. Army recruits are treated with respect. However, recruits are asked to perform at a high level. If recruits perform poorly, drill sergeants try hard to make them perform well. Physical and mental trials are part of what makes recruits good soldiers.

Think about this question long before you enlist. The military can teach you to perform a job. More importantly, the military also can teach you a lot about yourself. However, you need to be willing to put all your efforts into the choice you've made.

ARRIVAL AND NEW FRIENDS

You have enlisted in the army. Now you will leave for basic training. There are several army bases around the country that teach basic training courses to new recruits. The base to which you are assigned depends on what kind of assignment you have chosen.

Army basic training is taught to male and female recruits. They train together except for combat training. By law, women are not allowed in combat units. They

Where you are trained depends on what you've chosen to learn in basic training:

Air Defense Artillery—Fort Bliss, TX
Armor—Fort Knox, KY
Combat Engineer—Fort Leonard Wood, MS
Field Artillery—Fort Sill, OK
Infantry—Fort Benning, GA
Military Police—Fort McClellan, AL

Learning to climb and rappel builds confidence in army recruits.

often serve in support units. These are groups that assist combat units behind the fighting lines. However, non-combat specific training is co-educational.

Before basic training courses begin, recruits spend a week getting to know the military. This happens at the Reception Battalion.

When recruits arrive at the reception battalion, they are greeted by a sergeant. He is responsible for getting recruits settled in and teaching them the basics. Learning the basics is called orientation. As a recruit, you will learn many things from this sergeant. However, this sergeant will not be your basic training drill sergeant. You will meet your drill instructor during the second week. This first sergeant will only be with you for the first week.

U.S. Army Ranks

General of the Army
General
Lieutenant General
Major General
Brigadier General
Colonel
Lieutenant Colonel
Major
Captain
Lieutenant
Sergeant
Corporal
Private

A sergeant is the highest-ranking non-officer in the army. Sergeants are the military personnel who train recruits. U.S. Army basic training courses are taught by men and women.

ORIENTATION WEEK

Orientation week at the Reception Battalion helps recruits prepare for training and later military life. This is called processing. Some of the Reception Battalion processing includes:

- Uniform issue and fitting
- Filling out personal history forms
- Getting an identification (ID) card
- Eye and dental checks
- Haircut

Orientation week covers what a recruit needs to know about sending letters to relatives, using medical facilities, and what to do for fun. As a recruit, you will be told about the medical benefits available to your family. This includes life insurance. Being in the military means there is a possibility that you will be involved in combat. In combat, there is a chance that you may be killed.

Also during orientation, a recruit learns what is expected of him for the next eight weeks. There are rules of conduct (how to act) to follow. As a recruit, you must take classes in barracks (where recruits live and sleep) upkeep and personal cleanliness (hygiene). There are physical training classes and also drill (marching) classes.

Learning to Live the Army Way

Be prepared to wake up at 4:30 a.m. For the next eight weeks, this is the life of a recruit. If you have an alarm clock, you may want to set it to wake you up earlier than 4:30. When wake-up call is given, thirty to forty young men are rushing to only ten sinks, three showers, and four toilets. It is better to get there first.

Afterward, you will line up in the dark and head off to breakfast. It is a long wait because there are many people. Standing in line waiting for your meal is a good time for you to meet people. Look around and notice all of the different

Army recruits meet people from many different places across the country.

faces. Listen to all the different voices. The other recruits come from all over the United States. Get to know your fellow recruits.

In the military, you can get paid either twice a month, or once at the end of each month. During your processing, you will be issued a two-hundred-dollar credit card. You may use the card to buy things while on post. The money you charge will be taken out of your first paycheck. Of course, you can bring your own money with you to basic training. However, the army recommends that you bring just enough for travel purposes.

With your credit card, you may purchase items you forgot to bring, such as a toothbrush or shaving cream. Such things are purchased at the shoppette. This is a grocery, department store, and gift shop all in one. Also available in the shoppette are prepaid phone cards, with telephones nearby. You'll want one of these to be able to call home to your parents or a friend.

Orientation week is a recruit's chance to find out everything about military life other than combat training. Don't be afraid to ask questions about religious services, leave (vacation) rules, or visitors. This is the time to learn about each of the services available to you. Don't worry, though. If you missed something, you will be able to find it out later. However, once basic training begins, your free time will be limited.

Training Recruits

Following orientation week, recruits enter basic training. As a recruit, you will be assigned to a platoon within a company. A platoon is a small army unit. A platoon includes thirty to forty soldiers. A company has three or four platoons.

As a recruit, you will be trained for all combat tasks by a drill sergeant. All drill sergeants are tough men and women. They have been trained to train recruits. Recruits need tough training to make them into tough, fighting soldiers. However, your drill sergeant is also someone to respect. His position in the army is one of trust and responsibility. He has gotten to this position through dedication and hard work. You must respect that hard work because you have yet to prove your value to the military. The drill instructor will teach you to work hard, gain

Physical training builds physical toughness.

confidence in yourself, and work with your fellow recruits as a team.

You will learn these skills by taking classes. There are different classes for different skills. You will learn physical fitness, weapons use, self-defense, and hand-to-hand combat. Later in basic training, you will learn first aid and battle strategy.

All basic training courses are given Monday through Saturday. Sunday is a recruit's day off. A recruit's personal time is limited, so Sunday is a good time to catch up on personal business. This includes doing laundry and writing letters. Recruits often perform extra work to catch up or get ahead in their training.

PHYSICAL FITNESS TRAINING

Being physically fit is a large part of succeeding in basic training. As a recruit, you will have physical fitness training every day. This training starts after breakfast following the 4:30 A.M. wake-up call.

Recruits run as a group. The drill sergeant runs alongside the platoon. He sings army songs as you run, and you repeat them. You may have heard such songs from watching a movie or television show. These songs help to set a running pace. Such songs also help recruits to set a marching pace. Recruits must learn to march in step. This builds self-discipline and teamwork.

Soldiers learn to march together in basic training.

Your run ends at a big field. Here you will join other platoons for exercise drills. Again, the drill sergeant leads these exercises. You will learn how to stretch your muscles properly. Then you will do push-ups and sit-ups. You finish each morning's exercise drill with

19

a two-mile run. The total time for your physical training will be about one and a half-hours. You will follow these rituals for the next seven weeks.

HAND-TO-HAND COMBAT TRAINING

Hand-to-hand combat training teaches recruits how to fight without using firearms. As a recruit, you will learn how to hurt an enemy using kicks, punches, and choke holds. Some of these fighting moves will teach you how to disable an enemy. Such training includes boxing techniques and martial arts moves.

Recruits also must learn how to use knives against enemies. Knives are effective weapons against enemies during hand-to-hand combat. There are specific ways to hold and use a knife during hand-to-hand combat. This course will show you how to use and care for your knife.

SELF-DEFENSE TRAINING

Being in the army is not just about attacking. Soldiers also must defend themselves. Self-defense training teaches recruits how to defend themselves during hand-to-hand combat. During self-defense training, you will learn how to block punches, kicks, and choke holds. Defending yourself in hand-to-hand combat can be a matter of life and death. Listen carefully and practice the moves taught to you.

WEAPONS TRAINING

Every army and each soldier knows how to use a variety of weapons. Rifle, bayonet, and grenade training are a large part of a recruit's basic training. As a recruit, you will be required to master each weapon you are taught to use during basic training.

Rifle

All recruits should be expert shots using a rifle.

More hours are spent on the rifle range than on all other courses but one. Only physical fitness training takes up more of a recruit's training time.

Carrying (bottom) and handling a rifle (top) are basic tasks all recruits learn.

The basic training marksmanship course uses the M16A1 combat rifle. This rifle is the standard issue of all U.S. combat soldiers. As a recruit, you will learn how to shoot this rifle with deadly accuracy. You also will learn how to take this weapon apart. You take a weapon apart to clean it. You will learn how to properly clean and maintain your rifle under all conditions. Sometimes you will be in the field on a training mission. Your rifle is what keeps you from being killed by the enemy. Having a clean rifle ensures your ability to fight back.

Bayonet

A bayonet is a thirteen-inch blade that fits on the end of a rifle. Often, recruits are afraid of becoming injured during bayonet training. However, bayonet training is not as dangerous as it may sound. Recruits use old car tires as "dummy enemies" against which they practice stabbing techniques.

Bayonet practice shows recruits the proper way to use this weapon against an enemy.

The bayonet is the last weapon you can use before hand-to-hand combat.

Grenades

As a recruit, you will learn about the different types of grenades used by the army. There are smoke grenades, which shoot smoke to hide soldiers and vehicles from enemy sight. There are also grenades that hurt enemies but do not kill them. These are called concussion grenades. Concussion grenades make loud sounds that affect an enemy soldier's ability to hear and move quickly. Finally, there are grenades that kill. These hand-held bombs are the size of a baseball but are a little heavier. There is a timer inside each grenade. When a pin is pulled at the side of the grenade, the timer starts. When the timer counts to six, the grenade explodes. The explosion shoots out metal pieces that can disable or kill an enemy. As a recruit, you will first practice with dummy

Learning to throw a hand grenade makes a soldier an important part of any army fighting team.

After training with "dummy" grenades, recruits are tested with live grenades.

grenades. You will learn how to throw them correctly. Once you learn this, live grenades are used to show you the damage they can cause. You must pass a grenade test. This test takes place on a special course. Here you must throw live grenades at targets. Becoming an expert at using grenades is important to each recruit.

FIRST AID

Many hours are spent doing first aid training. Being a soldier is dangerous business. Soldiers can get hurt in combat. If every recruit knows something about first aid, each will be able to help the others.

As a recruit, you will be taught basic first aid. You will learn how to clean and bandage a wound. You also will learn how to wrap a sprained or broken bone. Such skills will allow you to help yourself or a fellow soldier. Once aid is given, a wounded soldier can be taken to base for more complete medical care.

Every basic training course is important to each recruit's development. However, the greater goal of each course is to teach teamwork among the recruits. Teamwork is what soldiering and the military is about. Without teamwork, no battle or war can be won. Teamwork during basic training is not only about teaching recruits to fight as a group.

Team Development

Teamwork comes from caring for each member of a platoon. This caring is shown in many different ways. As a recruit, you will have the chance to help other recruits succeed in areas where they may have been failing. For example, if you are having trouble properly wrapping a sprained ankle, one of your fellow recruits who knows how can help you. Learning the proper way to wrap a sprain will allow you to pass the first aid course.

The same is true for each basic training course. Weapons training requires practice. If a recruit does not hold a firearm correctly, he will not be able to hit the target. Maybe you are already an expert shot. You can help your fellow recruit to understand how to hold his rifle correctly. As the weeks and the courses progress, each member of

Learning to work as a team is the most important skill any recruit will learn during basic training. One teamwork test is for recruits to carry logs in a race against other recruit teams.

a platoon will have the chance to help another. When a platoon is able to work together, they are able to become an effective team.

CONFIDENCE COURSE

The confidence course is a perfect example of teamwork in action. The confidence course is designed to help recruits overcome their fears of heights and danger. The course has wooden towers that have large gaps between them. Connecting the towers are rope bridges recruits must cross. Another challenge is to climb twenty feet high up a tree trunk. Though these are challenges for the individual to tackle, all recruits are rooting for each other to complete the challenge. Having a group of your friends calling on you to "Go for it!" and "Come on!" will help you to overcome such fears.

OBSTACLE COURSE

The obstacle course is where recruits must run through, crawl under, and climb over things. As a recruit, you will have to climb up high walls. You will crawl beneath barbed wire. You will run across logs set over trenches. There are rope ladders to climb, and log bridges to cross. All of these obstacles must be conquered. It will be up to you to help your buddies through the course. Many times, recruits will be afraid and will need your support to succeed.

The obstacle course trains recruits to get around, over, or through places they may see during battle.

ROAD MARCH

During the fourth week, recruits go on several four-mile road marches. As a recruit, you carry a backpack with all of your gear. Some of your gear includes a tent, changes of socks and uniform, and a rain poncho. You wear your camouflage uniform and helmet. Your canteen is filled with water. Your backpack and gear weigh nearly 60 pounds.

During the four-mile road march, your platoon marches in single file. Half of you march on the left side of the road. The other half march on the right side of the road. You will be able to see your buddies as you march. It may be a hot day, and you may be tired. Seeing your fellow recruits struggling as you are will push you to continue and succeed. There is always one recruit who is having a tough time. You may have to raise your voice to remind him that he can do it. Much of this fourth week will be spent road marching.

Road marches begin with recruits dressed in full combat uniform and carrying a rucksack packed with equipment.

TEAM SPIRIT

As a recruit, you will notice yourself transforming from an individual to a member of a team. The team is your platoon. You are part of a unit that works together and plays together. On your days off you will spend time with your fellow recruits. And why not? You've made friends that might be friends for life.

Final Test and Graduation

In the final phase of training, recruits go on a field training exercise. This exercise will use everything a recruit has learned during basic training. The field training exercise lasts for two days. As a recruit, you will experience the closest you can come to battle conditions without going to war.

The field test starts with a six-mile road march. Your platoon will then be sent deep into the woods. You and your teammates will have to find checkpoints within the forest. Only your compass and a map will safely get you to these points and back to camp.

At camp, you will put up a tent with a friend. You will eat packaged army food. These are called MREs (Meals Ready to Eat). There are different entrées in each MRE, such as Beef

A field test requires recruits to use all the skills that they have
learned throughout the six weeks of basic training.

Stroganoff, or spaghetti and meatballs. If you don't like your entrée, try trading with a buddy.

During the exercise, you will experience fake gunfire and bombs. The gunfire and bombs are used to show recruits how loud battle can be. Under these loud conditions, soldiers can make mistakes. The only way to prepare for battle is to train in conditions that simulate battle. As a recruit, your ability to perform under hard conditions will prove to both your platoon and yourself that you are a soldier.

Battle simulations bring to life conditions under which soldiers may fight.

After a successful field exercise, it is time to celebrate. Your training has paid off! The drill sergeant will be happy. He may allow you to have pizza and sodas in the barracks.

At the end of a successful battle simulation, recruits have earned the right to feel happy and celebrate.

Such a luxury was a serious no-no during training. But your training is done. You are about to graduate.

GRADUATION

The last week of basic training prepares recruits for graduation. As a recruit, you will practice marching skills with your drill sergeant. He will lead you and your platoon onto the parade field. You will be alongside many other units like yours. They, too, will be graduating with you on the last Friday of basic training.

You spend many hours practicing both marching and saluting. During the breaks, you will have time to reflect, as a group, with your drill sergeant. He will want to know from you what you thought was done right and what was done wrong during basic training. This is your chance to open up to your drill sergeant. He wants to know how he can improve his training of future platoons. Most recruits say basic training is too easy. They want to make it tougher for the next group of recruits. There's a lot of pride among the soldiers.

Family and friends are accepted at graduation ceremonies. The army likes to show off its newly graduating troops. Have your family make hotel reservations early. Hundreds of people will attend the ceremony.

Today is the day! You parade onto the field with all of the units. Your brass and shoes are

*U.S. Army basic training graduation is a time for honor
and praise for a job well done.*

shined. Families and friends see you on the
field. This is the moment for which you have
been training. One of your platoon mates will
be selected to carry the platoon flag. Some people will be called out of formation to receive
awards. They receive them for having helped

their classmates during training. They have put in extra time. You may be one to be called. Awards are based on leadership skills and performance during training. After the speeches are made, you march past the bleachers back to your barracks. Parents have rushed there before you. Your drill sergeant marches you in, facing your barracks. He yells "Platoon halt!" He does an about face and tells you what a pleasure it was to train you. Then he yells, "dismissed." You have become a U.S. soldier.

These newly graduated U.S. Army soldiers share a moment before the camera.

41

New Words

air defense artillery cannons and rocket
   launchers used against airplanes and other
   enemy aircraft

armed forces name given to include each of
   the four military branches: army, navy, air
   force, marines

armor any covering used for protection

basic training a training course used by
   each military branch that teaches recruits
   basic duties and skills

bayonet a thirteen-inch blade that fits on the
   end of a rifle

company a group of about 150 soldiers
   formed by three or four platoons

confidence course a physical training
   course that requires recruits to climb high
   structures to get used to such heights

enlist to join a branch of the armed forces

field artillery cannons and rocket launchers used against other ground troops

field training a practice battle or war exercise in which recruits use skills that they have learned

first aid medical assistance used to treat an injured person

grenade a hand-held bomb that can be thrown and is timed to explode after several seconds

infantry a group of fighting soldiers used for ground battles

obstacle course a physical training place where recruits learn how to climb over or crawl under things

orientation getting to know and understand

something with someone's help

platoon a group of thirty to forty soldiers

recruit a newly joined member of the armed forces

recruiter someone who helps a person to join an organization

soldier a member of an army

For Further Reading

Green, Michael. *The United States Army (Serving Your Country)*. Mankato, MN: Capstone Press, 1998.

Hole, Dorothy. *The Army and You*. Parsippany, NJ: Silver Burdett Press, 1993.

Kurtz, Henry I. *The U.S. Army*. Brookfield, CT: Millbrook Press, 1993.

Moran, Tom. *The U.S. Army*. Minneapolis: Learner Publishing, 1990.

Resources

Organizations
United States Army Training Center
Fort Jackson, SC
803-751-6719
http://jackson-www.army.mil

Web Sites
United States Army Homepage
http://www.army.mil
Official site of the United States army. Contains recent news about military events and has links to many other military organizations.

United States Army Training Center
http://jackson-www.army.mil
An introduction to the United States Army Training Center in Fort Jackson, South Carolina. Learn the history of the training center. Also includes links to other military sites.

Index

About the Author

Gene Gartman is a thirteen-year veteran of the U.S. Army. He lives in Columbia, South Carolina.